The Star of Beth[illegible]em

Michael Hearns

Copyright © The Star of Bethlehem, Michael Hearns, 2017

All rights reserved: no part of this publication may be reproduced, stored in a retrieval system, or transmitted in any form or by any means, electronic, mechanical, photocopying or otherwise without the prior written permission of the publisher.

ISBN 978-1-9162844-7-0

Self-Published in Dublin, Ireland in 2020.

The moral right of the author has been asserted

A copy of the CIP entry for this book is available from

The Copyright Library of Congress, Washington DC, USA

and Trinity College, Dublin, Ireland.

www.sevenbiblewonders.com

Table of Contents

Tables

Introduction

The first Christmas day was on February 26th in the year 6 BCE for that has turned out to be the date when Jesus was born. This is the deduction that was drawn when an archive of ancient astronomy was recently uncovered for it gave the technical specification of a bright star over Bethlehem. After centuries of speculation the great secret has been at last revealed about the Messiah's date of birth and the identity of that mysterious star. This new discovery will have major repercussions in the Christian world but it is not as simple as changing Christmas day from December to late February. Christmas is a major festive season where it is a bonanza time for shopping and it is followed immediately by the New Year's jostling spree in retail sales. The possible side effects of the new discovery are thus enormous and they even affect Santa where he could have to readjust his time schedule to arrive with bags packed each year at Christmas Eve before the 26th of February. Whatever the consequences the new date will have on Christmas the magnitude of the discovery with the date of the birth of Jesus is the relevant issue.

The key to unlocking the mystery of Christ's birth was with the phenomenon, which became known as the Star of Bethlehem There were several theories doing the rounds about the identity of the star of which a triple conjunction with the planets of Jupiter and Saturn in the year 7 BCE was perhaps the most popular. A triple conjunction is where Jupiter and Saturn come in close alignment together on three occasions over the period of several months. That occurrence in 7 BCE was quite rare because the triple conjunction happened against the backdrop of the constellation of Pieces, which was a spectacle that only happens every 794.4 years.[1]

In ancient times the stars and planets were a source of breaking news stories, which the astrologers at the royal courts studied for signs of ills or omens. So when the Magi enquired from King Herod about the new born king because they had seen his star, they were speaking from an educated insight about the heavenly phenomenon. It was also noticeable that the

---

[1] Reference Common errors in Star of Bethlehem Planetarium Shows by Mosley Griffith Observatory LA USA

Magi were using astrological terminology and so they would have known that Jupiter was associated with the anointing of kings while Saturn was viewed as the saviour of Israel. These should have been familiar terms in the context of a prophesised Messiah who would be a redeemer and saviour of the Jews. That the coming together of those two planets was in the constellation of Pieces also told of a new beginning where the constellation of the fishes was coming into ascendancy for the next two thousand years. The signs in the sky would soon take hold when fishermen lined up to be apostles to a new radical preacher.

It was strange where the pagan worship of astrology featured in the very first page of the New Testament where the Magi linked a star to a new born king. Astrology was so out of place with the religious ethos of scripture. Likewise with the Magi for who were those star gazers who came to herald a new born king of the Jews? The traditional interpretations of Mathew's gospel are almost sacrilegious where three pagans from an alien culture such as Babylon or Persia broke the greatest news story in Christendom. In a faith that has been subject to so many conspiracy allegations one would wonder why the early church fathers had not erased or amended the tell-tale astrology link between a star and the birth of Jesus from Mathew's gospel. It shows that the Magi and the star were of tremendous importance in the story of Jesus.

Those were the puzzling aspects surrounding the star, which I faced when I set out to investigate its identity. The investigation took on board the various predictions of a Messiah by the prophets and it led to a trail whose stepping stones went back through the mystifying words of scripture. Luke's gospel had referred to Joseph and Mary going to Bethlehem at the time of a census. It was therefore remarkable when the stepping stones led to a census of the Israelites on the exodus out of Egypt. Under methodical examination, the census proved to be a camouflage where the analysis showed that the numbers were in fact the days of a solar calendar. This was a rare but revolutionary finding especially as it showed that the Bible had harboured a secret archive of astronomy.

There was more tantalising evidence to follow where I noticed that the names of six of the tribal leaders who partook in that alleged census were singled out for special attention in the gospels, particularly at the birth of Jesus. It was like the joy of opening a Christmas stocking because the total of the numbers for those six tribes added up to the exact same period as when a triple conjunction repeats itself every 794.4 years. The evidence kept mounting for there were also some very pertinent periods, which were cited in the gospels about the pregnancies of Elizabeth and Mary. Elizabeth got pregnant and for some peculiar reason she hid herself away for five months. Then Mary got pregnant and went to visit Elizabeth who was in her sixth month of pregnancy. Mary stayed with her cousin for around three months and then went home and that was about the time when John was born. Six months later Jesus was born at Bethlehem. Those timing periods matched up exactly with the time line of the triple conjunction in 7 BCE and with those of another rare planetary occurrence, which immediately followed where there was a triangulation of Jupiter, Saturn and Mars on February 26th in the year 6 BCE. Indeed, the timing from the date of the first phase of the triple conjunction of Jupiter and Saturn on the 27th May in 7 BCE to the date of the triangulation of the three listed planets on the 26th February in 6 BCE was exactly nine months and, of course, this was the same as the period of Mary's pregnancy.

The biblical prophets had predicted a Messiah but nobody knew that they had also charted the timing of his birth in the stars. This remarkable feat of astronomical engineering was charted several hundred years before the birth of Jesus and it cast a heavenly mantle over him. The gospel writers obviously new of the cosmic time schedule when they factored in the time periods surrounding the births of John and Jesus. For Jesus to be born within that forecasted time period with the conjunctions of the planets would have been nothing short of miraculous. It is the scientific evidence, which Christians have long awaited – the evidence to show that the prophets were divinely inspired with their predictions. For the Jewish fraternity however it will be a new dawn for they still live in expectation of a Messiah. But the findings show that not only was Jesus born in the right place but he was also there at the right time as forecast by the biblical prophets.

The investigation begins by examining the clues in the gospels relative to the predictions of the prophets. From there the trail expands out into the associated small print of the original predictions. Like the clues of a cryptic crossword the puzzling phrases are encountered but the stepping stones eventually lead to the exodus out of Egypt where an enormous census of twelve tribes was conducted. It was obvious that the population size was totally exaggerated yet nobody looked under the bonnet of scripture to see why.

Chapter 1

Predictions and Clues of a Messiah in the Small Print

The predictions by the biblical prophets of the coming of a Messiah played a major part in uncovering the unique archive of astronomy. Those prophets emerged as a *tour de force* on the biblical horizon after the ninth century BCE and played a fundamental role in shaping righteous thinking. They were perceived to be visionaries who were divinely inspired and acted with an independent voice. Instead of commanding armies with swords, those prophets stood alone and wielded power by a higher almighty force. Their elevated status as anointed ones came from what were deemed to be visionary trances, where they predicted the future of the Jews together with the activities or demise of their enemies. The greatest prophecy in the Old Testament was of the coming of a Messiah and snippets of the forecasts were evident with several of the prophets. As a result the Jews would have been continually on the lookout for this expected Messiah and a close watch kept checking for signs that would identify him relative to the details the prophets had forecast. So when Jesus came the gospels recorded the fulfillment of several predictions of the Messiah beginning with Mathew's gospel in the very first page of the New Testament.

The Magi came enquiring from King Herod and asked him: "*Where is he that is born King of the Jews? For we have seen his star in the east and have come to worship him.*"[2] Herod consulted with the priests who referred to a prediction about a ruler to be born in Bethlehem. But there was also a prediction by a prophet named Balaam back at the time of Moses. Balaam had predicted the coming of a ruler and he had linked the event to a star where he stated: "*A star will come out of Jacob a sceptre will rise out of Israel... A ruler will come out of Jacob.*"[3] Thus, the gospel

[2] Matthew's Gospel Chapter 2:2

[3] Book of Number's Chapter 24: 17.19

statement had encapsulated the words of Balaam in the dialogue with Herod and the Magi.

Thereafter the predictions in the gospels were numerous and the one the priests interpreted for Herod that identified the place of the Messiah's birth was by Micah: *"But you o Bethlehem, in the land of Judah, are by no means least among the rulers of Judah; for out of you will come a ruler who will be the shepherd of my people Israel."*[4] The quote built on the earlier prediction by Balaam about a ruler but the prophet Micah went on and identified the place of origin of the Messiah as Bethlehem and of course Jesus was born in Bethlehem. Isaiah was the next prophet in line and his unusual prediction stated: *"Therefore the Lord himself shall give you a sign; Behold, a virgin shall conceive, and bear a son, and shall call his name Im-man-u-el."*[5] This sentence was accepted in the gospels as Isaiah having predicted a Messiah who would be born of a virgin. I have since read that there was a mistranslation and that the word 'virgin' was cited instead of the original Hebrew Bible wording with "a woman shall conceive."

After the Magi had visited Jesus they were told in a dream to go home by a different route so as to avoid alerting King Herod of the whereabouts of the infant child. When Herod realized he was duped he ordered the massacre of all new born boys. This caused the gospel authors to invoke a prophecy from Jeremiah where he had written: *"Rachel weeping for her children, and would not be comforted, because they are not."*[6] Rachel was the wife of the founding fathers of the Israelites who was named Jacob and the couple formed a central part of the earliest Jewish family genealogy. Jacob was the patriarch of the twelve tribes of Israel and his name featured in Balaam's prophecy. Traditional sources had interpreted Rachel's weeping as being her spirit crying for the baby victims of Herod's massacre of the new born baby boys. However, there were other good reasons for the spirit of Rachel weeping especially because of what happened to her own two children who were Joseph and Benjamin? Her son Joseph was sold into slavery in Egypt by his own step-brothers and Rachel died in labour giving birth to her second son Benjamin. And of all places Rachel died in Bethlehem where Jesus was born.

---

[4] Book of Mathew Chapter 2:6, Book of Micah Chapter 5:2

[5] Book of Isaiah Chapter 7:14

[6] Mathew's Gospel Chapter 2, Jeremiah Chapter 31

By questioning the traditional standpoint of Jeremiah's prophecy about Rachel weeping for her children some other issues came to notice. The quote had inadvertently introduced Benjamin because he was also born to Rachel at Bethlehem. After that I became aware that the names of several of his stepbrothers were also evident at the birth and circumcision of Jesus or in other parts of the gospels. At the circumcision of Jesus there was a man called Simeon in attendance together with Anna who was identified as a descendant of the tribe of Asher. Jesus was born unto the tribe of Judah and later in the gospels the names of Zebulun and Naphtali were cited.[7] The name of Ephraim was also cited in the gospels where Jesus visited the city of Ephraim.[8] Those seven names with Simeon, Asher, Judah, Zebulun, Naphtali, Ephraim and the implied name of Benjamin were part of the twelve tribes of Israel. It made me wonder was there anything significant as to why they were specifically listed or inferred in the gospels.

The study of the Gospels progressed from there and the next puzzle to be investigated was a reference in Luke's gospel to a census. Historians have tried to date the year of Christ's birth relative to this census but the timing details were too confusing. This is where a fundamental departure from the traditional outlook arose and the clue was again with Rachel. The pertinent scene was outlined at least fifteen hundred years beforehand and it was in the Book of Genesis. In the scene Rachel was sitting on her camel's saddle beneath which she had hidden some false images, which she had stolen from her father Laban. Her father came searching for the images and searched her tent. He obviously wanted to search the camel's saddle but Rachel indicated that she could not stand up because she had her period. In biblical times a woman's menstrual cycle was seen to be comparable with the monthly cycle of the moon which is 29 ½ days long.[9] The menstrual cycle thus introduced an undertone of lunar time and it was remarkable therefore to find that the name of her son Benjamin who was born at Bethlehem signified 'the son of days.'

Things progressed from there where I was on a trip and staying in a hotel and came across a copy of the Gideon Bible in my room. On flicking through the pages I stopped at the first chapter of the Book of

---

[7] Mathew's Gospel Chapter 4:15:16

[8] John's Gospel 11:24

[9] Reference Rachel Elior, *The Three Temples*, Page 55 Published by Littman Library 2005

Numbers where a census of the population of men who came out of Egypt was held. Unlike the KJV of the Bible with its textual display of the numbers such as with say "twenty seven," it showed the figures in numerical format such as with the number 27. On browsing through the numbers I was surprised to see that eleven of the figures ended with a double zero, which was extraordinary. The norm in real life is that the numbers from a population tally will be evenly distributed with the unit digits spread over the range zero to nine. My immediate reaction was that the first three digits of those twelve numbers were multiplied by one hundred thus accounting for why they ended in a double zero. I went down through the list and came across Benjamin who had silently featured in the gospel clue about Rachel weeping for her children. It was an eye opener because the tally count for his tribe was given at 35,400 men. Having an interest in astronomy I knew that the lunar year was 354 days long and here was one hundred times that number. Was this finding a mere coincidence or had Rachel led us from Bethlehem where her son Benjamin was born at the time of a mysterious census into the Book of Numbers where a census was held. And lo and behold the numbers of Benjamin's tribe were the equivalent of one hundred lunar years. No wonder the meaning of Benjamin was known as "the son of days."

This was a curious finding with Benjamin but ancient Jewish logic operated on the principle that there had to be two witnesses to substantiate a case to be factual. Therefore, the research moved on from there to see if there were any other sightings of a recognizable orbital time period on the horizon. I read the various prophecies in the Old Testament and also read the adjoining text associated with the original predictions to try and place the forecasts in context. After all that was what a detective would do in trying to cover all of the angles in an investigation. In this regard there will be several references which had not featured previously with Gospel commentators and these will be highlighted in blue print. I will begin with the small print, which adjoined the quote about Rachel weeping and the text was as follows: "***I am a father to Israel and Ephraim is my first born.***"[10] It was a complete falsehood because Ephraim who was Rachel's grandson was not the first born for his brother Manasseh was older than him. Even at this early stage of the investigation I felt that this mistake

[10] Book of Jeremiah Chapter 31

was like a prospecting license to follow Ephraim and see why he was fingered out by such an error.

I soon found that Isaiah's prophecy relevant to a woman shall conceive also had some unusual small print in the adjoining text with reference to Ephraim as follows: "***Within three score and five years shall Ephraim be broken, that it be not a people.***"[11] This is where it is important to observe the body language for the period of 65 solar years was also the same length in days as 67 lunar years and in reality, both shared the same birthday. It also should be noted that the first age of the patriarch Enoch was 65 years and he supposedly died when he was at the notable number of 365 years old.

Those seemed to be potent clues but I also wondered why had Isaiah stated ***that it be not a people, which can be broken open?*** The statement by Isaiah was followed later in the text where it went on to state: **"*In that day, in every place where there were a thousand vines worth a thousand silver shekels.*"**[12] The reference to a thousand vines worth a thousand shekels had not featured previously with investigators but soon it would prove to have a deeper meaning which was numerically time related.

There was one final clue to be considered with reference to the flight into Egypt by the holy family in order to escape the slaughter by King Herod. It outlined in Mathew's gospel how this departure would in turn fulfil the prophecy from Hosea as follows: "Out of Egypt have I called my son"[13] I then read the original prophecy from Hosea as follows: "*When Israel was a child, then I loved him, and called my son out of Egypt".*[14] It appeared as if Mathew was using poetic license when he referenced Hosea because the association with Jesus in the prophecy was so tenuous? Instead, the prophet had named Israel as a child, which was in fact Jacob. Jacob was not in Egypt as a child so there was a need to look further to see who was the son who was called out of Egypt. Just two sentences down from the quote in Hosea the small print in the reference continued as follows: ***"I thought Ephraim also to go, taking them by their arms; but they knew not that I healed them."***[15] The earlier reference to Israel (Jacob) and now to Ephraim was more realistic in the

[11] Book of Isiah Chapter 7:8 KJV
[12] Book of Isaiah Chapter 7:23 Revised KJV
[13] Mathew Gospel Chapter 2:15
[14] Book of Hosea Chapter 11:1
[15] Book of Hosea 11:3

quotes from Hosea because Jacob went to live in Egypt in his old age and there he met for the first time his grandson Ephraim. The part of the phrase "but they knew not that I healed them" was interesting because to heal someone you bandage or cover up their wounds. Was this reference to ***I healed them*** a hint of a cover up?

In the quotations so far, four of the prophets had singled out Rachel's grandchild Ephraim for special attention. The quest now was to check in scripture for signs of something which ***can be broken with 65 years*** and ***"that it be not a people,"*** with the expectation of finding ***a 1,000 vines worth a thousand silver shekels.*** Included in the quest was Jeremiah's reference to ***Ephraim as a young boy who is perceived to be the first born.*** There were also those references from Hosea ***linking Israel with Ephraim, coming out of Egypt*** and ***taking them by the arms.***

The Sign of the Cross

With those clues on board it was easy to detect where the quote from Hosea featured. It involved a high profiled scene with Jacob, his son Joseph and two grandsons Manasseh and Ephraim. In the scene, Jacob laid the groundwork where he fretfully referred to Rachel and notably how he had buried her in Bethlehem. He then sought to bless the two boys. Joseph led his two sons towards Jacob ensuring that the older Manasseh went to the right hand side and the younger Ephraim to the left hand side of their grandfather. However, Jacob deliberately crossed his arms to bless the younger Ephraim with his right hand while he blessed the older Manasseh with his left hand. Blessing the younger Ephraim with the right hand went against tradition but Jacob justified his actions by stating that Ephraim would be greater than Manasseh. In effect, Jacob had made the sign of the cross by overlapping his two arms and of course the cross was to become associated with the ever lasting image of Jesus. The clues in the small print with Hosea of ***Ephraim, Israel, Egypt and taking them by the arms*** had borne fruit and remarkably, even at that early stage in biblical history, the cross was the sign to follow.

Because the clues from the prophets had all but dried up I employed the aid of a biblical search engine to home in on more listings of Ephraim. When I entered the name Ephraim and hit the return key the search engine stopped at Chapter 1 in the Book of Numbers. It was there that Moses had conducted a census of the twelve tribes of Israel. On a trail that had begun with the reference to an unknown census it was rewarding to find the search had borne fruit where it had led to a census of the twelve tribes of Israel. It was the second encounter with this census for the clues with Benjamin had also led to this population tally where the numbers of his tribe at 35,400 was the equivalent value of one hundred lunar years. Was there another surprise finding in store?

The names of the twelve tribes were all listed with their related numbers in the census. However, Ephraim stood out because he appeared before his older brother Manasseh. Jacob had forecast that Ephraim would be greater than Manasseh and this was true where the numbers for the younger son totalled 40,500 men as compared to 32,200 men for the older brother Manasseh. I moved on to look at the second census of the tribes, which was held at the end of the forty years in the wilderness when all but two men from the first census had died. I found that Manasseh had regained his rightful place and appeared before Ephraim in this second census. This change of position seemed unimportant until I tried entering the numbers of both censuses onto a spreadsheet. It was an eye opener because the names and numbers for Ephraim and Manasseh formed a crossover as follows:

1st census			2nd Census	
Ephraim	40,500		Manasseh	52,700
		×		
Manasseh	32,200		Ephraim	32,500

The changeover of the names and numbers with both men formed into a crossover so the sign of a cross had again surfaced. Rather than go into to much numerical detail at this stage it is essential to let the cat out of the bag by performing computations, which were gleaned from the biblical instructions. When the numbers of Ephraim were added together and then halved the result was as follows:

40,500 + 32,500 = 73,000 ÷ 2 = 36,500

The sign of the cross had led into a maze behind the computations to reveal a very high visibility number where the average for Ephraim's two censuses came to 36,500. This number was the equivalent of one hundred solar years in whole days.

By following the clues from the prophets the trail had led to the two censuses of the tribes of Israel to reveal a result which as Isaiah had stated ***"that it be not a people."*** The reference by Isaiah relating to 65 years was loaded for it pointed to Enoch whose first age was 65 years. But Enoch's final age was given at 365 years and here was that number in the display for Ephraim as 36,500. Isaiah had stated ***"that it be not a people"*** and finding the number 36,500 and the earlier number of 35,400 suggested that instead those numbers were the days of a solar calendar. There was also another reference and it was by Hosea, which further qualified the findings where the prophet referred to Ephraim stating ***"The iniquity of Ephraim is bound up; his sin is hid."***[16] The prophet had specifically named Ephraim and as outlined, the solar related time of 36,500 with Ephraim was bound up and well hidden. Rachel had pointed the way like a signpost where the numbers of her son Benjamin and her grandson Ephraim represented the moon and sun respectively in the two data banks, which had been paraded as two censuses.

[16] Book of Hosea Chapter 13:12

Chapter 2

The Four Calendar Time Charts

The Bible does not give the real picture of events in the world of the Israelites. In recent centuries scholars have discovered from a detailed study of the entomology and syntax of the first five books of the Old Testament that there were at least four main writers whom are identified as J, E, D, and P. A fifth writer R redacted the four scripts and combined them together as if they were just one script. In his book, "*Who Wrote the Bible*?" Professor Richard Friedman outlined how the script was changed and large tracts of text were inserted such as with the story of Noah and the flood where there were two different versions written back to back.[17] Strangely, the insertions included hosts of numbers including practically the whole Book of Numbers. Part of those numerical insertions included those two censuses of the tribes of Israel.

This revision of the Torah took place possibly six hundred years after Moses. Therefore, the censuses were obviously devised with something far more important in mind. In both censuses the men numbered more than six hundred thousand, which would have made a total population of two million people when wives and children were included. Such large numbers together with their families would have compared to the population of a modern big city. Yet they were all fed by manna or breadcrumbs from heaven and spouts of water from a rock, which was no better than a village pump.

The sheer logistics of counting such numbers would have been overwhelming. A sample of the textual recordings of the numbers read as follows: From the descendants of Reuben forty and six thousand and five hundred, from the descendants of Simeon fifty and nine hundred and three hundred, from the descendants of Dan three score and two thousand and seven hundred and so on until the total of six hundred thousand and three thousand and five hundred and fifty was listed. Full marks to

---

[17] Friedman, Richard Elliot, *Who Wrote the Bible*? New York: Harper, 1997.

anyone who can figure out the numerical list for it was Reuben at 46,500, Simeon 59,300, Dan 62,700 and the total of the twelve tribes came to 603,550. It was similar for the second census where the monotony continued until a total of 601,730 was listed in textual format.[18] No wonder few people ever bothered to give the numbers in that format a second glance. Thankfully the Gideon Bible had presented the figures in the numerical format such as with a total of 603,550.

Common sense tells us that this could not have been the outcome of a census because in any tally, the numbers end with random digits distributed in unit figures from zero to nine. The size of the alleged population size was also too enormous to fit in with the storyline and also eleven of the numbers ended with the bizarre anomaly of a double zero. I outlined earlier that these peculiar observations raised an interesting question. Were the first three digits listed for each tribe multiplied by one hundred for that would account for the last two digits ending with a double zero? For instance the tribe of Benjamin at 35,400 men was 354 multiplied by one hundred. Another time period had emerged for the lunar year is 354 days long.

The twelve tribes were supposed to have been the descendants of Jacob's ten sons and two grandsons. Jacob was also called Israel. We were told that Moses held a census of those twelve tribes of Israel at the beginning of the second year on coming out of Egypt. Thereafter, the storyline tells us that God got fed up listening to the moans of the freed slaves and declared that they would die before reaching the Promised Land of milk and honey. Therefore a second census was held at the end of the forty years in the wilderness to count the men of the next generation when all but two from the first census had died. Those two men were Joshua and Calum. The second census introduced some more

---

[18] Our present arithmetic differs greatly from ancient times where we have developed technicalities such as a positional base ten system, decimals together with an invisible zero to conduct computations. Therefore, we have to place ourselves in the ancient landscape and understand the arithmetic which was used by the biblical writers. The Egyptian and Babylonian systems of arithmetic have survived and are well known in academic circles. It is also known that the ancients used fractions for detailed examples of this ability was found on the Egyptian Rhind papyrus, which ironically was dated to the time of Moses around 1,300 BCE. Without delving deeper into this intricate field of ancient numbering system it should be sufficient to alert the reader of the different symbols, notations and calculation methods, which were used in olden times.

anomalies where for instance the numbers of Gad at 40,500 was the same as for Ephraim in the first census. Likewise, the numbers for Asher in the second census was the same as those of Naphtali in the first census. The same listings of numbers were either careless scribal errors, which is hard to accept from those devout masters or else it was downright extraordinary. Either way, it was another nail in the coffin for the notion of these sets of figures having been two censuses.

I gathered from the instructions in the Book of Numbers that the captured land of Canaan would have to be divided up between the twelve tribes in proportion to their numbers. Did this mean the numbers from the first census or those from the second census? The fairest solution appeared to be to add the numbers of each tribe together from the first and second census and then halve the total in order to get the average number for each tribe. The potential of having two time periods with Benjamin and Ephraim prompted me to do some analysis on the other figures. I added up the numbers of Jacob's first wife Leah sons in the first census. Their totals came to 292,200. As a time period the number converted to eight hundred solar years. Again the period looked to have been multiplied by one hundred especially as the base period of 2,922 days or eight years was very important in astronomy and it is known as the octaeteris.

The finding with the octaeteris was an encouraging next step in the quest and soon another oddity caught my attention there was something unusual about the arrangements of Leah's five sons. In their midst were the numbers of Gad even though he was born to a different mother. I then found that by adding on the numbers of Gad to Leah's five son's numbers the new total introduced the corrective synchronizing factor between the solar calendar year of 365.25 days and the actual solar year of 365.2422 days. Simply put I added the numbers of Gad at 45,650 to the total of Leah's sons at 292,200 and the new total converted to 925 years to an accuracy of less than one day when divided by 365.2422. This was a remarkable finding because that degree of clarity with solar time was thousands of years before its time. For instance the Julian calendar began in 45 BCE and it had a 365 ¼ day solar calendar, which went out of date by one day every 130 year approx. It was finally corrected by the Gregorian calendar in the 16th century CE to reflect the true solar year of 365.242 days. Was this finding with the correct solar calendar just a fluke coincidence or did the ancients know precisely the true length of the solar year?

While conducting further analysis I added up the numbers of the tribes in the average group one by one beginning with Reuben, then Simeon, then Gad, Judah, Issachar, Zebulun and then Manasseh. I was watching the calculator and saw the total after adding Manasseh came to 365,240. It was the equivalent of one thousand solar years to within two days. To achieve the exact target of one thousand year two more men would have been required. And lo and behold two men, Joshua and Caleb, had survived to be two extra in addition to the second census. This made the total complete at 365,242 for the number of days in one thousand solar years. It was the evidence I had been looking for where it showed that the biblical astronomer knew the true length of the solar year.

Thus the final link in the predictive chain had emerged to fulfil what Isaiah had referred to with the figure of one thousand vines and shekels: ***That wherever there could be a thousand vines worth a thousand shekels of silver.***[19] A vine tree produces a crop of grapes every years and taking the word in that context, one thousand vines equated to one thousand years. In the Book of Exodus, each descendant of the twelve tribes from the original census had to donate a half shekel towards the upkeep of the sanctuary. Those donations would equate the one thousand years to the one thousand shekels. I.e. Before the numbers were halved the total for those seven tribes in sequence added up to the equivalent value of 730,480 or two thousand years. There now was sufficient evidence from the analysis so far to indicate that the numbers, which were paraded as two censuses were instead the days of a solar calendar.

The two censuses have stood through time like the pyramids, while onlookers from every generation passed by unaware of the purposeful design within their secret interior chamber. The words of scripture were taken by the faithful to be the infallible word of God while the numbers were perceived as being no more than rigid zombies serving a superficial role; devoid of any significant purpose. At this stage there was sufficient evidence to press ahead and update the terminology in order to avoid confusion between references to censuses of men and calendar days. Therefore, the first and second census will be retitled the first and second calendar charts. The totals of the numbers from those two charts will be

[19] Book of Isaiah Chapter 7:23 Revised KJV

called the third calendar chart. In turn, the average of the totals from the third chart will be labelled the fourth calendar chart as is shown in the table below. Because we are dealing with ancient arithmetic it is essential to state that numerical data was very different in antiquity but don't worry for I have presented the finding using our contemporary numerical symbols and mathematical methods.

This fourth calendar chart was where most of the calendar indices were archived so take a while and study how it was so simply hidden from public view. Those biblical scribes had basically apportioned the total of a peculiar long time period into twelve segments of what I have termed the fourth chart. After that things go in the reverse order. It seems that the scribes doubled each segment of the fourth chart to get the third calendar chart. Then the divided the third chart into two separate parts, which we now have labelled the first and second calendar charts. (These were paraded as the original two censuses of the twelve tribes) In that way the sacred calendar in the fourth chart was hidden behind those computations. In effect it was a secret chamber where an archive of precious information was stored in the 4th chart. So perfect was the method of concealment that it escaped the prying eyes of millions for over two thousand years.

Because time periods had been detected, the censuses were retitled as the **1st chart** and **2nd chart**. The total of the numbers in both charts was entitled the **3rd chart** and the average of the numbers was entitled the **4th chart** as shown in Table 1.

Table 1: The Four Calendar Time Charts

Names in	1st Chart		Names in	2nd Chart	3rd Chart	4th Chart
1st Count			2nd Count			
Reuben	46,500		Reuben	43,730	90,230	45,115
Simeon	59,300		Simeon	22,200	81,500	40,750
Gad	45,650		Gad	**40,500**	86,150	43,075
Judah	74,600		Judah	76,500	151,100	75,550
Issachar	54,400		Issachar	64,300	118,700	59,350
Zebulun	57,400		Zebulun	60,500	117,900	58,950
Ephraim	**40,500**	✖	Manasseh	52,700	84,900	42,450
Mannaseh	32,200		Ephraim	32,500	73,000	**36,500**
Benjamin	**35,400**		Benjamin	45,600	81,000	**40,500**
Dan	62,700		Dan	64,400	127,100	63,550
Asher	41,500		Asher	**53,400**	94,900	47,450
Naphtali	**53,400**		Naphtali	45,400	98,800	49,400
Total	**603,550**		**Total**	**601,730**	**Total**	**602,640**

The scribes gave each segment the name of a tribe, which in turn were named after the ten sons and two grandsons of the patriarch Jacob. Thus we had twelve groupings. There was more to follow because Jacob had in fact twelve sons and these were born to four different mothers. His first wife Leah had six sons while his second wife Rachel had two sons. There were also two hand maidens Zilpah and Bilah who had two sons each by Jacob. Leah's son Levi and Rachel's son Joseph did not feature in the future twelve tribes. Instead Joseph's two sons Ephraim and Manasseh took the places of Joseph and Levi. Thus there were twelve mini groupings with the twelve men's names and four extra larger groupings with the four mother's names. To make things easier it is intended to stick to those names of the men and the mothers during the forthcoming analysis.

Mapping Biblical History from Isaac to Jesus

Notice how the numbers of Reuben, Simeon, Gad, Judah, Issachar, Zebulun and Manasseh all in sequence added up to **365,240**, which was the equivalent of one thousand solar years to within two days as shown in Table 2.

Table 2: The Strategic Calendar in the Fourth Chart

Leah	Leah	Zilpah	Leah	Leah	Leah	Rachel	Rachel	Rachel	Bilah	Zilpah	Bilah	
Reuben	Simeon	Gad	Judah	Issachar	Zebulun	Manasseh	Ephraim	Benjamin	Asher	Naphtali	Dan	
45,115	40,750	43,075	75,550	59,350	58,950	42,450	36,500	40,500	47,450	49,400	63,550	
												I
← 365,240 Days or 1,000 Years →							← 476 Years →				174 Years	S
30 CE						970 BCE				1,446 BCE	1,620 BCE	A
												A
Jesus						Solomon				Exodus		C

Thereafter, the evidence was detected to suggest that the remaining five modules in the fourth chart were to be rearranged for they served a particular purpose. In the new formation the four modules with Ephraim, Benjamin, Asher and Naphtali in sequence added up to the period of 173,850 days. That period converted to 476 years. It soon became apparent that this calendar should be overlaid on biblical history dating back from Jesus when he was about thirty years old.

It outlined in the Gospels that John began to preach in the 15th Year of the reign of Tiberius Caesar and that was reckoned by historians to be in August of 29 CE. (Luke 3:1) Jesus began to preach six months later which would have been in 30 CE. By superimposing the one thousand years on biblical history beginning with the anchor point in 30 CE, the timeline led back to 970 BCE. That year was another anchor point because it was the year when Solomon was crowned king.
The next period with 476 years on the calendar led back from when Solomon was crowned king in 970 BCE to 1,446 BCE. Lightening had struck twice because it outlined that Solomon began to build the temple in the 4th year of his reign, which was 480 years after the exodus out of Egypt. (1 Kings 6:1) Therefore, it was 476 year from when Solomon was crowned king back to the exodus. (480 – 4 = 476 years) In effect, that 4 year period had acted like a tongue and groove overlap to join the two periods of 1,000 years and 476 years in sequence. Finally, the calendar dated back to 1,620 BCE and from Luke's and Matthew's genealogies, it proved possible to identify that Isaac was born in that year.

Throughout the remainder of this research work there will have to be a double speak when referring to this biblical solar calendar. This is necessary because the whole calendar was framed and structured disguised as two censuses. At the higher level were the four groups paraded as mothers with the names of Leah, Rachel, Zilpah and Bilah. Then there were the twelve groups of time periods in each calendar chart and these were identified as leaders of each tribe. There were also other elements of the calendar where the numbers were paraded as men who were slain for being disobedient during the forty years in the wilderness and of course, they affected the numbers in the calendar charts. For instance, the slain men reduced the population sizes and therefore their numbers had to be subtracted from the totals in the census charts and likewise from the calendar charts. In the forthcoming analysis it will be necessary to use the original terminology using men, tribes, mothers etc. for they were the recognizable elements of the instruction manual. But we now know that these men represented the days of a solar calendar and that is why the double speak will have to apply in order to carry out the laid down directions of the instruction manual.

The Secret Archive of Astronomy

Chapter 3

Jupiter and Saturn

Having identified that the numbers that were paraded as two censuses were instead the days of a solar calendar, the next task was to examine the charts to see if the jigsaw pieces could be assembled to reveal recordings of the luminaries. In the findings so far there were the equivalents of one hundred lunar years with the numbers of Benjamin and one hundred solar years with the numbers of Ephraim. There was also eight hundred solar years with the numbers of Leah's sons in the first calendar chart. This was followed by the display with one thousand years with 365,240 days from the numbers of Reuben down to Manasseh in the fourth chart. On further investigation I discovered that the numbers of Judah, Issachar, Zebulun, Manasseh, Ephraim, Dan, Asher and Naphtali in the fourth calendar chart added up to 433,200, which were one hundred orbits of Jupiter. The investigation therefore continues and begins by looking at a special feature, which pertain with the planets.

Planetary Birthdays

In the broader aspects of this research it was found that the planets had special anniversaries. Take for instance the first planet Mercury. Its orbit around the sun takes 88 days. However every seven years Mercury returns to its original spot in the sky and this can be vicwed where it actually crosses the face of the sun. The evidence suggests that the priests saw this occurrence with Mercury as the planets having an anniversary every seven years. With the planet Venus its orbit around the sun was every 224.7 days. After eight years Venus also crosses the face of the sun. Therefore, Venus also had an eight year anniversary cycle. An example of these anniversaries can be illustrated as follows. When you were born Venus would have been in a particular spot in the night sky. After that Venus would have carried on about its business of orbiting the sun over and over again. On your eight birthday however, Venus would have returned to the same spot in the night sky where it was on the day you were born. That is why I have termed these anniversaries with the planets as planetary birthdays.

From a simulation exercise I learned that Mars had a special birthday where it shared the same date with the solar year every 79 years. The exercise also showed that Jupiter practically shared a special anniversary birthday with the solar year every 344 years and every 1,554 years. With Saturn it was every 324, 383 and 707 years. In other parts of my research work on the tabernacle of Moses I found that the orbits of Mercury, Venus, Mars, Jupiter and Saturn had been encrypted into the dimensions of the structure.[20] This had been accomplished where particular surface areas in square cubits had the same numerical values as the orbits of those planets. It was also discovered that the special birthday for Mercury, Venus, and Saturn had been factored into the dimensions of the tabernacle. This placed those special birthdays on a sound biblical footing and showed that they were of major importance to the priests and prophets. Because the findings with these planetary birthdays were alien to our way of thinking I checked to see if there was evidence of these anniversaries from antiquity. It transpired that there was such evidence and it was found on Babylonian tablets dating back to the 4th century BCE.[21] The tablets had recordings of those periods with Venus, Mars and Jupiter together with various long periods for Mercury and Saturn. Therefore the simulation exercise of identifying those planetary birthdays was on a firm footing. Because the Jews were exiled in Babylon, it indicated that may have been where the biblical writers had acquired that knowledge of what I have termed birthday anniversaries.

The big breakthrough in this research work was the discovery of the solar calendar with the numbers, which were covertly paraded as two censuses of the tribes of Israel. There were more surprises in store where the biblical astronomers created side shows in the desert wilderness by having men slaughtered for disobedience so as to factor in numbers, which would produce different totals of time periods in the calendar charts. The research has revealed that the main purpose of the exercise was to display multiple orbits of Jupiter and Saturn in order to archive the technical coordinates of the mysterious heavenly phenomenon, which became known as the Star of Bethlehem.

---

[20] Reference *The Mystery of the Tabernacle*, 2015 at www.sevenbiblewonders.com

[21] Reference Hunger, Hermann, *Astral Science in Mesopotamia*, Brill 1999. P 202-205.

The Template Model of 1,597 Years

The exercise begins by revealing the template model of a time period, which was identified from one of the side shows that impacted on the solar calendar charts. In the sideshow, 14,700 men died of a plague and in a separate episode another 24,000 men died of a plague. Thus, there were two groups of numbers, which related to the plague. As such, it seemed like an invitation to carry out a computation exercise to see if there was a purpose for the men being slain. This is where the double speak applies for in effect the slaying of men was an exercise in subtracting their two sets of numbers from the first calendar chart. When the two totals were subtracted from the chart the result was as follows:

603,550 – 14,700 – 24,000 = 564,850

This new total of 564,850 for the first calendar chart was then added to the second calendar chart of 601,730 and the total divided to get the average values as follows:

564,850 + 601,730 = 1,166,580 ÷ 2 = 583,290

That number of 583,290 when applied as days proved to be 1,597 solar years. Therefore, by introducing the double speak exercise of having two sets of men die by plagues, the biblical astronomer had factored in the pertinent numbers to produce that overall result with 1,597 solar years.

Jupiter

It was discovered that the writers had factored in three appearances of the orbit of Jupiter in those sideshows where men allegedly died for being disobedient. There was an episode where 250 men had rebelled against Moses but curiously, there were two separate versions of the affair with two different punishments in the same story. In one episode the 250 men were swallowed up by an earthquake while in another version of the story, they were struck dead by lightning. The double speak applies where in the second alleged census the 250 men were referred to again as the counting of the second census took place.[22] Therefore, it appeared the

[22] Book of Numbers Chapter 26

scribes were pushing the number 250 before our nose for special attention. In the original story line, if the men had not been slain then they would have been still alive to feature in the second census. The question was what would be the effect on the calendar chart totals if the numbers had not been subtracted? By applying the men as days the inherent instruction meant adding the two appearances of 250 days to the total of the second calendar chart at 601,730 days. The result was 602,230 days. This number proved to be 139 orbits of Jupiter to the very day. This result turned out to be a prime example of how the biblical astronomers had created the sideshow scene with those numbers to factor in 139 orbits of Jupiter in the amended total of the second calendar chart.

The scribes were not yet finished with Jupiter for there was a whole series of sideshows, which involved the slaying of 3,000, 14,700, 24,000, 250 and 10 men in separate incidences together with a further four individuals who were slain for breach of the Sabbath or having sex with a foreigner. In the original story line, the 3,000 men were slain before the first census was counted while all the other men in the sideshow were slain after the census was conducted. To take this aspect on board it meant adding those 3,000 days to the first calendar total at 603,550 days and the result was 606,550 days. Thereafter, it was necessary to subtract the numbers of the alleged men who were slain, which we now know to be time periods in days. The result was as follows:

606,550 – 14,700 – 24,000 – 250 – 14 days = 567,586 days.

The outcome of 567,586 days proved to be 1,554 years to the very day. It was also 131 orbits of Jupiter to within seventeen days. It was a notable result because 1,554 years had an interesting feature with regard to those clusters of biblical sevens where it was twice the period of 777 years.

The third example with Jupiter arose from the totals of the men who came out of Egypt. Before any men were slain in the sideshows their total would have been as follows:

603,550 + 3,000 + 24,000 + 14,700 + 250 + 14 = 645,514

The total of 645,514 proved to be 149 orbits of Jupiter to within 41 days.

The biblical astronomer had thus factored in three examples with Jupiter into the calendar charts. In the first example above it showed how the numbers were introduced to change the overall total of the second chart to factor in 131 orbits of Jupiter to the very day. In the second exercise the scribes had factored in all of the numbers of the sideshows to give a result with the amended total of the first chart, which provided an example of harmonizing 139 orbits of Jupiter with 1,554 solar years. The third example revealed that the total number of the men who came out of Egypt at the exodus when expressed as days actually represented 149 orbits of Jupiter.

Saturn

The next part of the research work was to examine the figures in the gruesome side shows of men been slain to see if they were part of an exercise that included the orbit of Saturn in the calendar charts. We have already seen that one of the sideshows told a story about 250 men who rebelled against Moses. The Lord retaliated and these men were swallowed up by an earthquake. There was a repeat of the rebellion the men except in the second version the men were consumed by lightning. Heretofore, the two episodes with the 250 men were viewed as just one event but with different forms of punishments. To find out what the scribes were up to, the numbers in the first two calendar charts (were the two original censuses) were adjusted to reflect the actual outcome with one cast of 250 men who were slain in the sideshow. In reality, it meant that the 250 days had to be subtracted from the total of the first calendar chart at 603,550 days and the new total came to 603,300 days. The next step was to add this adjusted total from the first calendar chart to the total of the second calendar chart at 601,730 and then get the average value to form the fourth chart. The resultant total was 602,515 days. The new total of 602,515 proved to be fifty six orbits of Saturn to the very day. The evidence would suggest that linking multiple orbits of Saturn to 1,650 solar years in the equation above was an example that was given by the biblical astronomers to demonstrate how to correct a shortfall between multiple orbits of Saturn so that it could notionally share its anniversary with 1,650 solar years.

We have seen above how the totals of the men who came out of Egypt when expressed as days had proven to be 149 orbits of Jupiter. There was a second result pending from that total and it applied to Saturn. Before any men were slain in the sideshows their total that came out of Egypt would have been as follows:

603,550 + 3,000 + 24,000 + 14,700 + 250 + 14 = 645,514

The total of 645,514 proved to be 60 orbits of Saturn to within 38 days. It was an extraordinary result because 60 orbits of Saturn multiplied out to 645,552 days whereas 149 orbits of Jupiter multiplied out to 645,555 days a difference of only three days. It showed that the biblical astronomer had inserted a theoretical equation, which encompassed the nearest breakeven point in time when Jupiter and Saturn could practically share the same birthday as when the originally started their orbits 1,767 years 131 days beforehand.

Overview

The three examples with Jupiter and the two examples with Saturn showed that those planets were a coherent part of a biblical time line. As such they proved to be demo models in revealing the identity of the Star of Bethlehem. The prime example of those demo models was in the first chart where the original total plus the numbers from the side shows housed multiple orbits of Jupiter and Saturn in the one overall total. In fact, the total led to finding the closest point of equilibrium in time for those two planets coming together. The first chart featured again where its amended total with the numbers from the sideshows housed 131 orbits of Jupiter. There was a double aspect to this result in the first chart where it proved to be 1,554 years to the very day. This showed that the biblical astronomer had factored in an example of how to harmonize 131 orbits of Jupiter with 1,554 solar years. The revelations continued where the amended totals of the second chart housed 139 orbits of Jupiter. The final result was in the fourth chart where the amended total from with the number of a sideshow revealed 56 orbits of Saturn to the very day. It also had that double factor where it provided the means of harmonizing 56 orbits of Saturn with the total of the fourth chart at 1,650 solar years.

The overall results showed that the biblical astronomer was using the correct orbital periods for the planets of Jupiter and Saturn. The orbital period for Saturn is 10,759.2 days and for Jupiter 4,332.59 days. From the results it can be ascertained that the biblical astronomer multiplied the orbital period of both planets to get the theoretical values over long term periods. Those results with Jupiter and Saturn were the final straw in the defence line of those sceptics who would stubbornly refused to believe that the numbers, which were paraded as two censuses were after all, the days of a solar calendar.

There were side effects from these discoveries, which deserve attention. The slaughter of so many men by God and Moses has always bewildered scholars and the faithful alike. It went totally against the fifth Commandment of *thou shall not kill*. However, the findings have revealed that all those killings were fictitious and were orchestrated to insert the numbers of the secret calendar into the Torah. It is strange that the re-editors placed God and Moses in this compromised position but it may have been a ploy keep the followers in line by showing that God was ready to punish offenders.

The lambing season is in late February and this would appear to be the likely reason why the gospels tell us that the shepherds were in the fields at Bethlehem. Photo was taken in Doonamona in County Mayo, Ireland in late February 2017.

Chapter 4

The Star of Bethlehem

The scene was set to finally examine the vital orbital characteristics for evidence of the phenomenon that became known as the Star of Bethlehem. Kepler in the 16th century was the first to suggest that there was a triple conjunction with Jupiter and Saturn in the constellation of Pieces in the year 7 BCE and it thereafter became the likely candidate to have been the Star of Bethlehem. While trying to establish if this triple conjunction was a rare event I came across an article on the Internet by Mosley.[23] He outlined that nearly every 800 years (actually 794.4 years) Jupiter and Saturn begin a new cycle back at nearly their original position as measured with respect to the vernal equinox. Mosley stated that the conjunction which Kepler watched had occurred in essentially the same position 800 years before and 800 years before that. Mosley had clarified that the repeat period of the triple conjunction more precisely as occurring every 794.4 years.

The repeat performance of the triple conjunction bore a strong similarity with regard to my research work where it fell into the same category as the planetary birthdays and also with those five examples with Jupiter and Saturn in the calendar charts. Until now there was no way of astronomers knowing that the triple conjunction of Jupiter and Saturn was the Star of Bethlehem because there were no technical specifications to verify the issue. But there was light on the horizon where the biblical scribes had covertly given us five examples of how to illustrate multiple orbits of Jupiter and Saturn. Was it possible that the scribes had also factored in the technical specifications of the unusual sighting, which became known as the Star of Bethlehem? I worked on the presumption that those five examples with Jupiter and Saturn were the criteria the scribes had utilised for future generations to one day detect and identify that the triple conjunction of Jupiter and Saturn was the Star of Bethlehem. Therefore, I decided to apply the same criteria between the

[23] Reference www.ips-planetarium.org/?page=a_mosley1981

previous triple conjunction of Jupiter and Saturn and the triple conjunction in 7 BCE and then check for those details in the calendar charts.

Mosley had listed the time period back to the previous triple conjunction as 794.4 years and this was 794 years146 days. Therefore, the previous conjunction with those planets of Jupiter and Saturn in the constellation of Pieces before 7 BCE would have been in the year 801 BCE approximately. By starting at a common starting date in 801 BCE there would have been 27 orbits of Saturn at 795 years 131 days and 67 orbits of Jupiter at 794 years 281 days running in parallel until they both reached the year 7 and 6 BCE. Thus there were three possible parameters which the biblical astronomer may have applied to identify the Star of Bethlehem as Jupiter and Saturn coming close together and they were as follows:

Triple conjunction every 794.4 years	**=**	**794 years 146 days**
Saturn × 27 orbits	**=**	**795 years 131 days**
Jupiter × 67 orbits	**=**	**794 years 281 days**

The next step was to check the calendar charts to find if those three periods had been factored into combinations if the numbers. It would have been a daunting task and nothing short of a special computer programme would have sufficed to identify if there were any such combinations in the charts. However, the scribes had written in or had silently insinuated the names of seven tribal leaders in the gospels beginning at the birth of Jesus. Their collective numbers were matched against those three time parameters of the triple conjunction. The outcome was as spectacular as the triple conjunction itself beginning with the result in the second chart as follows:

Simeon + Judah + Zebulun + Ephraim + Asher + Naphtali = 795 Years 132 Days.

This first result compared to 795 years 131 days for 27 orbits of Saturn, which occurred between the triple conjunction in 801 BCE and its repeat performance in the year 7 BCE.

The next result was in the fourth chart as follows:

Simeon + Judah + Benjamin + Ephraim + Asher + Naphtali = 794 Years 147 Days.

The second result compared to 794 years 146 days between the triple conjunction in 801 BCE and the triple conjunction in 7 BCE.

With breath-taking precision two important parameters from the triple conjunction of Jupiter and Saturn every 794.4 years had matched up with six of the seven tribal names of Simeon, Judah, Ephraim, Asher Naphtali, Benjamin and Zebulun. One group was in the 2nd chart while the other was in the 4th chart. All that it required was to exchange Benjamin with Zebulun in both charts to create two of the recognisable periods relative to forming the multiple orbits of Jupiter and Saturn. The identity of the Star over Bethlehem was now on a scientific footing because the orbital details were to hand to verify it was that triple conjunction.

As already outlined six of the tribal names were clearly listed in the gospels while the name of Benjamin was silently insinuated. There were two other tribal names that were possibly insinuated in the gospels though their listings were ambiguous and those were with the names of Gad and Dan. There was no direct mention of Gad but instead there was a reference to the Gadarenes. I thought at first that the Gadarenes were from the tribe of Gad but I could find no evidence in biblical sources for this assumption. Likewise, there were two references to Daniel the prophet in the gospels but this could not be directly taken to mean the tribe of Dan. Even though those two references to the Gadarenes and Daniel the prophet in the gospels were very much at arms-length from the names of Gad and Dan I still decided to check the combination involving those two names coupled with the original seven names of the tribes?

The 67 orbits of Jupiter had not been accounted for relative to the identity of the triple conjunction at the time of the birth of Jesus. Therefore, I simply added up the numbers of the nine tribes for each of the first, second and fourth chart and subtracted the 67 orbits of Jupiter from their three totals. This made the computations much more manageable where I had only to check the remainder to see if six of the tribal numbers made up those multiple orbit of Jupiter. The outcome from the fourth chart proved to be as follows:

Simeon + Gad + Zebulun + Ephraim + Dan + Asher = 794 years 273 days.

The period of 794 years 273 days contained 67 orbits of Jupiter to within eight days. Those extra two names with Gad and Dan had yielded up the third parameter with 67 orbits of Jupiter to confirm the theory of the triple conjunction in 7 BCE having being the Star of Bethlehem.

The Birth Certs of John and Jesus

Now that the identity of the Star of Bethlehem was at last known it is time to examine the gospels and see if the particular time periods in months surrounding the conception and birth of John and Jesus bore a relationship with the triple conjunction in the year 7 BCE. Astronomers have calculated that the first phase of the triple conjunction occurred where Jupiter and Saturn came very close to each other on the 27th May of 7 BCE in the constellation of pieces. The two planets then parted but they came back close together on the 6th October 7 BCE. They again parted company but returned almost together on the 1st December 7 BCE. The two planets then went their own way and that ended the triple conjunction. But there was still a rare spectacle in sight where there was what Hughes called a 'fiery triangle' of Jupiter, Saturn and Mars around the 26th February 6 BCE on the border of Pieces and Aries.[24] Therefore, there were precise dates with the conjunctions of Jupiter and Saturn and the fiery triangle to try and match the timing of the events in the gospels.

We were told in the gospels that an angel called Gabriel visited an old priest named Zachary and foretold that his aged wife Elizabeth would bear a son. Elizabeth got pregnant and for some peculiar reason she hid herself for five months. Thereafter, we were told that the angel Gabriel visited Mary and she miraculously got pregnant from on high. Mary then visited Elizabeth and it was in the 6th month of her cousin's pregnancy. Elizabeth's baby jumped in her womb when the two women met. This was a similar occurrence to what had happened to Rebecca when the twins Esau and Jacob had stirred in her womb. Mary stayed with Elizabeth for about three months and that was about the time when John

---

[24] *Astronomical Thoughts on the Star of Bethlehem* by David W Hughes, P128-130 at https://books.google.ie/books?isbn=9004308474

would have been born. Meanwhile the Magi were on their way following a peculiar star.

Now let us match up those time periods in the gospels with those in the triple conjunction in 7 BCE and the massing of the planets together in February 6 BCE. Hughes pointed out that during late 8 BCE and early 7 BCE the planets of Jupiter and Saturn approached each other. Therefore, I have taken December 8 BCE to be the starting month of when Elizabeth got pregnant with her son John. She then hid away for five months, which brought the proceedings up to late April or the beginning of May in 7 BCE. What was so special about the five months in hiding by Elizabeth and was the period reflected in the triple conjunction? I found a reference that the movements of Jupiter and Saturn would have started to become noticeable in late April of 7 BCE because the two planets had come to within three degrees of each other and this was a limit, which would have applied over the course of the next eight months.[25]

Mary was visited by the angel Gabriel and it seems reasonable to suggest that the visit was on the 27th May 7 BCE when the first occurrence of the triple conjunction took place. Mary then visited Elizabeth and it stated that it was in the sixth month of her cousin's pregnancy. Mary stayed with Elizabeth for around three months, which would bring the proceedings up to sometime around the 27th August in 7 BCE. That would have also been the time when John was born. There was six months to go with Mary's pregnancy and that would have brought the events right up to the 26th February in 6 BCE. The dates matched up exactly especially with the nine months pregnancy from the 27th May 7 BCE to the 26th February in 6 BCE.

Jesus was born on the 26th of February in the year 6 BCE. That is what the findings indicate and the whole event with Mary's pregnancy was reflected in the heavens beginning with the conception of Jesus at the first phase of the conjunction of Jupiter and Saturn on the 27th day of May in 7 BCE. It ended with the massing of Jupiter, Saturn and Mars together on February 26th in 6 BCE. In reality the whole episode from the conception of the Messiah to his birth was written in the stars. It was a powerful method of mirroring calendar time down here on earth with the events in the heavens. A layout of the timing events with the dates of the conception and births of John and Jesus is shown on the diagram below.

---

[25] Reference www.space.com

Dating back in time from the first phase of the triple conjunction on 27th May 07 BCE would place the conception of John at around the 27th November in 8 BC and his birth on the 26th August 7 BCE. The chart shows the timing details with the dates of the conception and births of John and Jesus. The prime dates were plotted against the first phase of the triple conjunction on the 27th May when Jesus may have been conceived and continued to the spectacle with the massing of Jupiter, Saturn and Mars on the 26th February in 6 BCE when he was possibly born. It was a nine month period exactly and it was the deciding factor in selecting those two dates. Of course, superimposing those dates on each other was a subjective choice by me. But it was the biblical prophets who planned the sacred time line with ingenuity and so it behoves us to interpret their intentions by using the same degree of meticulous application.

The Birth Certs of John and Jesus Charted in the Heavens

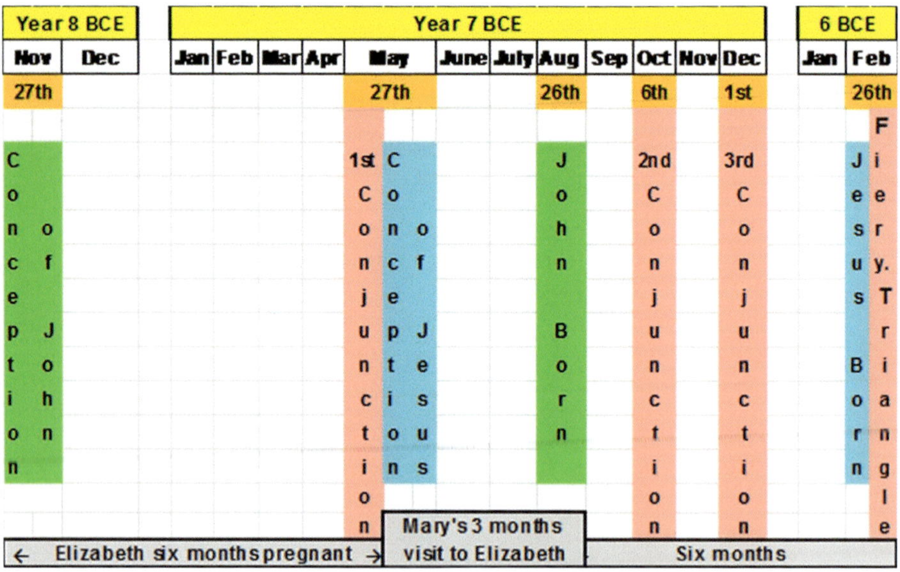

The result of showing the birth of Jesus having been on the 26th February in 6 BCE will see the conjunction timing details subjected to the most rigorous scrutiny. As such, more sophisticated software simulations may result in a slight variation with that date.

Chapter 5

A Star Would Come out of Jacob

Now that the identity of the Star of Bethlehem is known it is time to look at the bigger picture and see why the prophet Balaam had cast an oracle, which had predicted that a star would rise out of Jacob. Because Balaam supposedly lived at the time of Moses it was possible that his oracle referred to a previous triple conjunction back at the time of Jacob? The conjunctions with those planets Jupiter and Saturn before the year 7 BCE would have been in the year 801 BCE approximately. Before that the previous conjunction of those two planets would have been in the year 1,596 BCE. To see if Jacob fitted into the picture at that time it was necessary to examine the evidence and see if the scribes had left any clues on dating the time period.

The Two Genealogies

There were two separate links between Jesus and Jacob and those were with two genealogies in the gospels. The first genealogy was at the beginning of Mathew's gospel and it listed the men by name in forty two generations from Abraham forward to Jesus.[26] In Luke's gospel there was a genealogy which was even longer and curiously, it listed the men by name from Jesus back through the Bible.[27] It was thus an indication of dating events back in time. In the finer details with Luke's genealogy it listed all the men in each generation back to King David and thereafter onto Abraham and continuing on to Adam and then God. Abraham formed the fifty sixth generation back in time from Jesus. I poured over the two genealogies to see if I could establish a time line from the various ages that were listed for the men throughout the historical stories in scripture. Without labouring the details of the search all I can say is that I

[26] Mathew's Gospel Chapter 1.
[27] Luke's Gospel Chapter 3.

found several anomalies with the genealogies and also found the research was going nowhere with trying to add up the individual ages of the patriarchs.

Because there was no reliable calendar in ancient times the age the monarchs began to rule was the linage to map out the years and days. For instance it stated that it was in the fourth year of Solomon's reign he began to build the temple. However, I came across some unusual information on dating via ancestry and it applied to both the Egyptians and the Greeks. They assigned a set given age for each generation. E.g. the Egyptians had a system of applying three generations of their Pharaoh's in one hundred years, which was an average of 33 ⅓ years per generation for each monarch.[28] It seemed very odd to have every individual in the genealogy assigned a set time period yet it must have had merits in its day.

With this average generation in mind I did the arithmetic with Mathew's and Luke's genealogies and found a remarkable outcome. If the period of forty years was applied to each of the forty two generations in Mathew's genealogy there would be 1,680 years from Abraham to Jesus when he began to preach at the age of thirty. In contrast, if the period of thirty years were applied to Luke's genealogy there would also be 1,680 years back from the thirty year old Jesus to Abraham after fifty six generations.

Things just fell into place after that where the periods of thirty years and forty years were more than justified. This was where Jesus was thirty years old when he began his ministry. John the Baptist and all the Levite priests also began their ministry when they were thirty years old. In turn Luke's genealogy traced the Levite side of the ancestry of Jesus and it started by saying that Jesus was thirty years old. Three of the descendants of Noah were thirty years old when they became the father of their first son. And those three men had featured in Luke's genealogy. Therefore, it was laid out on the drawing board of scripture that thirty years would have applied to Luke's genealogy. The period of forty years was also well heralded in the Bible where King David and his son Solomon both reigned for forty years as did many other biblical leaders. In reality, the period of forty years was the royal lineage of the Israelites and Judeans while thirty years was the priestly lineage throughout the Old Testament.

[28] John Marincola, Lloyd Llewellyn-Jones, Calum Maciver, Greek Notions of the Past in the Archaic and Classical Eras, Edinburg University Press, 2012 p100.

The central piece of the jigsaw then fell into place where King David was crowned king at the age of thirty and he reigned thereafter for forty years. His ages were like a template for the two genealogy structures with the set time periods of thirty and forty years.

These two genealogies both formed links between the time of Abraham and the time of Jesus. Indeed, the men in both genealogies were like links in two chains between Abraham and Jesus. On re-reading about the events in Abraham's life it became very obvious that there were certain similarities between the events back at the time of Abraham and those at the time of Jesus. Just like with Jesus the birth of Abraham's son Isaac was predicted. This prediction happened when three men of God visited the ninety nine year old Abraham on the plains of Mamre. Abraham was originally called Abram. While dining under an oak tree the men foretold that his old barren wife Sarah would bear a son and their descendants would be as numerous as the stars in the heavens. Sarah was originally called Sari. Notice the choreography with Abraham beneath a tree whose yearly rings were being silently insinuated for a family tree. Sarah laughed in disbelief at such an absurdity of getting pregnant at her age of ninety years but she was chastised by God for doing so. The three men of God departed saying they would return again at that time of life. They did not return when Isaac was born but three wise men came visiting when the last in the line of the two genealogies was born at Bethlehem.

The similarities between the events at either end of the two genealogies continued at the end of the timeline where an old priest named Zachery was visited by an angel named Gabriel who predicted that his old barren wife Elizabeth would conceive and bear a son. This was where there was another repeat performance because like Sarah, Zachery expressed disbelief that his old wife could conceive. Sarah was chastised by God for her reaction to the prediction that she would conceive while Zachery did much the same but he was struck dumb for his lack of faith in God's almighty powers.

Thus it can be seen that there were similarities between both ends of the two genealogies but they never stood out so visibly before until a timeline began forming with those two genealogies. An abbreviated list of those two genealogies showing the two lists of names running in parallel with each other between Jesus and David is shown in the diagram. Then they both joined into a single stem, which ran between

David and Isaac and then Abraham. Because of space requirements, I could only list some of the names.

The Abbreviated Lists of Names in the Two Genealogies

The top genealogy from Luke mapped out the lineage of the Messiah in intervals of thirty years from Jesus back to Abraham. The bottom genealogy with Mathew mapped out the linage from Abraham to Jesus in periods of forty years.

Those two time lines with the two genealogies would have been hanging in thin air relative to the conventional system of dating the historical time line of the Bible. But thankfully, the gospel writers had catered for this eventuality where they left a firm set of references to anchor the timeline onto the events of the day at the time when John the Baptist began to preach as follows:

"*Now in the fifteenth year of the reign of Tiberius Caesar, Pontius Pilate being governor of Judea, and Herod being tetrarch of Galilee, and his brother Philip tetrarch of Ituraea and of the region of trachonitis and Lysanias the tetrarch of Abilene, Annas and Caiaphas being the high priests, the word of God came to John the son of Zacharias in the wilderness.*"[29]

From that quote it can be seen that Luke left enough details of which royals were in power to anchor the timeline to a particular year. Historians were of the view that the 15th year of the reign of Tiberius began in August 29 CE Jesus was six months younger than John and it brought the time line when he began his ministry to around March 30 CE.

Luke's gospel was very explicit where it gave the age of Jesus at thirty years and also where it led directly into the genealogy, which listed the men of each generation back to Abraham and thereafter to Adam and God.[30] All the evidence was in that chapter with Luke to tell us that Jesus

[29] Luke's Gospel Chapter 3:1-2.
[30] Luke's Gospel Chapter 3:23.

was thirty years old in the year 30 CE and that Luke's genealogy started back in time from that year. Therefore, the years 30 CE were the starting point to identify who in the genealogy featured back at the time of a previous triple conjunction of Jupiter and Saturn in 1,596 BCE.

I did the sums and found that by superimposing the thirty year period on every generation from Jesus back through the fifty five names of the patriarchs in Luke's genealogy the dating identified with Isaac in 1,620 BCE. [31]The genealogy had pinpointed Isaac who was the father of the twins Jacob and Esau. There was a feeling of De Ja Vu about that timing with the 1,595 BCE date for it was when the twins Jacob and Esau would have been conceived by their mother Rebecca relative to the triple conjunction date.

It was noticeable that there was peculiar incident recorded in scripture about what happened to Rebecca when she was pregnant. The two babies stirred within her and she was told by God that two nations were in her womb. Because Rebecca's conception took place around the year of the triple conjunction of Jupiter and Saturn, it made me wonder if the twins together in the womb were the metaphorical representation here on earth of those two heavenly bodies being close together. It was peculiar how it outlined about the birth of the twins where Jacob caught Esau's heel when Esau was born just before him. After that the two twins grew apart with Esau being a cunning hunter, a man of the fields while Jacob was a plain man who dwelling in tents. Similarly, Jupiter and Saturn were in close proximity at the time of the triple conjunction and after that they also parted company. By 7 BCE, the orbits of Jupiter and Saturn were six months apart and this was symbolised on earth where Jesus was born six months after John.

To reinforce the issue with the twins of Esau and Jacob having been the metaphorical representation of Jupiter and Saturn, a peculiar occurrence with twins also happened possibly sixty years later with respect to Luke's genealogy. It was important because every sixty years Jupiter and Saturn form a notable conjunction. A woman named Tamar conceived twins by an illicit encounter with her father in law Judah. When the twins were born one child stuck out his hand and the nurse tied a scarlet thread around it. The baby withdrew his hand and the other baby

---

[31] It should be noted that the CE era began in year 1CE and the era BCE began in the year 1 BCE. This was due to the position that there was no year zero when the dating system of Anno Domino AD was devised.

was then born first. With Rebecca, one twin caught his brother's heel while one twin stuck out his hand with Tamar thus bringing twins and a possible link to the sixty year cycle of Jupiter and Saturn to our attention.

The similarities of the events that happened back at the beginning of the time line and those at the end of the time line were an important part of linking the two ends of that lengthy period. At one end Jacob and Esau had stirred in Rebecca's womb whereas John jumped in Elizabeth's womb when the pregnant Mary visited her as if the two babies were being reconciled. Jacob caught Esau's heel when the twins were born whereas the foot was also insinuated where John had referred to Jesus saying "*I indeed baptize you with water; but one mightier than I cometh, the latchet of whose shoes I am not worthy to unloose:*"[32] At the beginning of the time line saga three men from God visited Abraham while at the end three wise men visited Jesus. Rebecca had come to Isaac riding on a camel while John wore camel skin thus indicating that it was the end of the line relative to a dead camel. Esau was a wild man of the fields while John lived on locusts and wild honey in the wilderness.

The pinpointing of the years 1,620 BCE for Isaac with Luke's genealogy was not a lone swallow for it was supported where the time line in Mathew's genealogy was in the same vicinity. But there was even a more dramatic third witness where the time line with Luke's genealogy from the thirty year old Jesus back to Isaac matched up exactly with the total of the solar calendar dating back to 1,620 BCE as in the fourth chart as outlined earlier.[33] It therefore followed that the findings with multiple orbits of Saturn and Jupiter in the amended totals of the calendar time charts had indicated that the biblical astronomer had theoretically projected those orbits back from or to the time of Isaac. That the two planets mapped out the timeline through the heavens was a wonder to behold from the prophets and it cumulated with the birth of Jesus at the time of a mysterious star and his royal anointing by the Magi. Their gifts of frankincense and myrrh introduced the concept of the tabernacle into the scene of the nativity because they were also the spices used to anoint the holy structure. It set the scene for the tabernacle to be utilized later in place of the tomb to explain the events surrounding the resurrection of Jesus.

---

[32] Luke's Gospel 3:16

[33] Reference Michael Hearns, *The Messiah Immortalised in Time* at www.sevenbiblewonders.com

Heaven and Earth Embroidered Together

Was the Messiah Predicted or Contrived?

There is evidence to suggest that the concept with the Messiah came into focus with the rise of Jewish mysticism around the time of the exile in Babylon. It was then that the biblical writers covertly re-edited the Torah and inserted the sacred calendar. An air of expectancy of a saviour to come was fostered and hints about his philosophy and encounters were given by the prophets including his birth at Bethlehem. However, when this saviour would come seemed to be at God's will. But now we have the calendar and it shows that Jesus lived at the same time as set out by the prophets on the timetable. Does this place the prophecy and calendar dating in the realms of the paranormal? For instance, how could the prophets centuries before Jesus, set out the time when the Messiah would be born and the year when he began his preaching career in what became the year 30 CE? The reams of literature written about Jesus could wallpaper the heavens but with this calendar, the writing was on the wall.

- Either the prophets were divinely inspired when they plotted out the meticulous timetable to date the coming of a Messiah and as Christians believe, Jesus was the son of God.

Or

- The Messiah was contrived by the prophets and Jesus was chosen and tutored to be the anointed one by the elite priesthood in order to fulfil the prophecies.

Either way, Jesus was in the right place, Bethlehem, at the right period on the timetable to be the predicted Jewish Messiah.

The second option if true was no doubt well intentioned for all the evidence in the gospels clearly shows that the policy was to give hope to the poor and inflicted who were at the bottom rung of the social class. By following in the footsteps of Jesus, the impoverished could look forward to the freedom of a blissful life in a heaven hereafter beyond the stark reality of a final curtain in an earthly grave. Alongside this ray of hope was the long term vision with a philosophy to engender peace, justice and equality that eventually formed the cornerstone of our modern democracies. And now for the first time there is the scientific evidence mapped out on calendar time charts for everyone to adjudicate if the narrative with the Messiah was in the realms of the paranormal.

Conclusion

Christmas day should be celebrated on the 26th February. It is the inevitable conclusion from the investigation into the phenomena, which became known as the Star of Bethlehem. The new evidence reveals that the biblical prophets had projected a sacred time line from the birth of Isaac around the year 1,620 BCE and it stretched down through the generations to Jesus. The earthly version of the time line was laid out in two genealogies and they ran precisely in parallel with that secret solar calendar charts over that lengthy period. Within the confines of that solar calendar were the indices of Jupiter and Saturn thus casting a heavenly mantle over the earthly realm below? The highlight of the time line was with a triple conjunction of those two planets in the year 7 BCE and it cumulated with a massing together of Jupiter, Saturn and Mars on the 26th February in the year 6 BCE. In essence, the biblical prophets had projected the coming of the Messiah in a divine sense where they had written the glorious path of his incarnation in the stars. It was a magnificent feat of astronomical engineering, which elevated the persona of the Messiah onto a heavenly divine realm.

The outcome is far reaching and particularly so for the Jewish congregation who are still awaiting the expected Messiah. The facts are that not only was Jesus in the right place at birth but he also was born at the right time as was projected by the prophets. There are also major consequences for the Bible. After centuries of confusion and debate about those incredible numbers in scripture the puzzle has now been resolved. Those numbers were not bizarre old ages of the patriarchs or the enormous sizes of two censuses. Instead they were the years and days of a solar calendar. It has also been shown that the slaughter of men in those side shows was not an act of vengeance by an angry God but part of the elements of an instruction manual to create particular orbits of the Jupiter and Saturn. The numbers lay on the surface of the biblical books while the solar calendar lay in the womb of scripture encompassing the Messiah to immortalise him in time.

To place the findings with the Star of Bethlehem in context it is necessary to give a summation of the overall research results. It is like a "*once upon a time story*" where I inadvertently ventured into examining some of the strange lists of numbers in the Bible from a mathematical standpoint. Never did I realise that it would become a research project, which would spread out over sixteen years to date. While studying the numerical data I performed calculations and noticed that dividing some of the numbers by 365.242 days to convert them to solar years revealed several notable time periods. To advance the investigation further it meant having to enter the various sets of numbers onto spreadsheets and conduct computations and checksum tests. In the process I uncovered many more examples of recognizable time periods. However, the results were disjointed and spread all over scripture so there was a lot of work to do to join all the jigsaw pieces together in order to tell the greatest story never told. .

It was like finding a large archaeological site and starting with a trowel to scrape off the soil and see what lay beneath the surface. On the vista of the alluring site there were ruins of a beguiling tower of Babel together with Jacob's ladder and the scene with Elijah's fiery chariot. These displays had one thing in common where they were describing encounters, which were reaching to the heavens. In addition, Noah's ark sailed upwards towards the heavens and the Magi's star was in the heavens above Bethlehem. The theme from the biblical writers about reaching to the heavens was obvious and suddenly here were the snippets of records to suggest that those prophets had a degree of scientific knowledge of astronomy.

The real breakthrough came when I unveiled the framework of a solar calendar from the numbers, which were paraded in disguise as two censuses of the tribes of Israel. It was an amazing discovery and one that academics will find hard to accept especially after centuries of intensive scrutiny of the Bible. From there the image of Jacob's ladder took shape where the time charts from the solar calendar contained alignments of the planets stretching to the heavens. In essence, the planets formed the rungs of the ladder in ascending and descending order. Next was the story of the Tower of Babel and notably it was in the same chapter as the incredible ages of Noah's generations. Noah was told to increase and multiply and that was an invitation for me to add and multiply the numbers in those same ages. The outcome showed a theoretical gateway to the constellations of the Zodiac. A purpose for the story of the Tower of Babel had emerged.

There was a riddle in the Book of Genesis concerning the first age of Noah and the first age of his son Shem, which introduced an anomaly of two years. This enticed me to analysis the timing details in the flood story because they might have a bearing on solving the puzzle. The analysis showed that the very precise timing details conformed to a formula involving the measurement of time in periods of 777 days. The analysis identified that the ark was travelling forward in time with the solar year but back in time in accord with the star year. A star year is how time is measured when sailing at sea and it is plotted by reference to a fixed star. The discovery showed that a biblical astronomer had plotted out the tiny difference in minutes between the solar and the star year possibly to illustrate an example of mortal time on earth and divine time in the heavens. This tiny difference between solar and star time is a simple element of today's astronomy but it may have been seen as a divine window to the stars by the superstitiously minded people in biblical times.

The scraping with the trowel continued and the next part of the research work was with the holy tabernacle. While entering the numerical details from the Book of Exodus onto a spreadsheet I noticed that three of the weights of gold and silver treasures in ancient talents and shekels had the same values as some of the heavenly orbits. The notion of a treasure trail beckoned and it prompted me to check the dimensions of the tabernacle for evidence of more time periods. It was an exercise in figuring out the earliest form of a flat pack instruction manual. However, it turned out to be a rewarding exercise where the numbers in square cubits of the surface areas and square areas of the holy structure had the same values as the orbits of the planets. There were also many more recognizable time periods in those findings. A litmus test using a larger size for the tabernacle tent failed to produce time periods and this exercise proved the findings with the planets involving the smaller tabernacle tent size were authentic.

The next part of the discovery ventured into the paranormal. It again involved the symbol of Jacob's ladder but it progressed further when I found that seven of the rungs were formed with the planets, which cannot be seen with the naked eye. And current opinion is that the ancients did not have telescopes. Those remarkable findings included three outer dwarf planets, which were only discovered between 2,003 and 2,005 with the aid of space age technology. Ironically, I uncovered the numerical coordinates of those three outer planets in the Bible in the same fourteen month period as they were discovered in outer space by astronomers. It transpired that the combined total of the orbits of the seven planets, which cannot be seen with the naked eye proved to be the same as the total of the numbers in the first solar calendar chart at 603,550 days. What made the finding even more sensational was where the instructions in the Book of Numbers were to have those numbers arranged in the shape of a huge solar cross. Therefore, there was a metaphysical dimension to the cross, which placed a mystical aura over the crucifixion of Jesus.

There were other discoveries such as how the indices of the special 777 day formula for measuring long time periods in years were ingeniously encrypted into the numbers of seven burnt offerings in the Bible. The research continued from there to reveal these findings on the Star of Bethlehem and the date of the birth of Jesus.

It appeared that I had effectively uncovered the biblical NASA space agencies set of astronomical records beneath the silt of the archaeological site of scripture. After years immersed in numerical data I finally got the space to become aware that there was more than digging for further pieces of trinkets in the sands of time. It was always going to be a daunting challenge to place all the pieces together and identify what the overall picture looked like. All the data seemed to point to the prophets where they had predicted the coming of a Messiah. What went unknown however was where the seers had also the information on astronomy to immortalise their prodigy in the metaphysical ether of time. The prophets charted a time line from the founding fathers of Abraham, Isaac and Jacob through the heavens with the orbits of Jupiter and Saturn and it stretched down to Jesus at the time of a bright star. The biblical astronomers were sitting somewhere in the middle of the time line where they possibly lived at least 500 to 700 years before Jesus. Their predictions told about a Messiah to come and how he would open up a new kingdom in heaven above. Jesus came along at the time of the predicted star and his extemporary role of preaching justice, equality and fraternity made him a role model to fulfil the expectations of what had been forecast by the prophet's centuries beforehand.

What changes everything was where the biblical prophets have now been shown to have possessed a vast knowledge of the heavens, which would seem to be beyond the capabilities of mere mortals to acquire at that stage of engineering development. This may sound like science fiction but the records of those far out dwarf planets are there in the calendar charts to support that statement. Then take a look at the combinations of the numerical data within the solar calendar charts and see the ingenious way the data matrix was constructed. Add in the findings that were obtained from the tabernacle. Include the magnificent jigsaw display of time periods, which lay behind the story of the flood. Those enigmas were masterful works of numerical wizardly and they appear to be beyond the ability for mortals to create back in biblical times. These are the issues for congregations to contemplate when they look for signs that there is a God.

Now pause for a pensive moment of reflection

Bibliography

Common errors in Star of Bethlehem Planetarium Shows by Mosley Griffith Observatory LA, USA. www.ips-planetarium.org/?page= a_mosley1981

Elior, Rachel, *The Three Temples*, Published by Littman Library 2005

Friedman, Richard Elliot, *Who Wrote the Bible?* New York: Harper, 1997.

Hughes, David W, *Astronomical Thoughts on the Star of Bethlehem* at https://books.google.ie/books?isbn=9004308474

Hunger, Hermann, *Astral Science in Mesopotamia*, Brill 1999. P 202-205.

Marincola, John and Llewellyn-Jones, Lloyd, Maciver, Calum, *Greek Notions of the Past in the Archaic and Classical Eras*, Edinburg University Press, 2012.

McLeish, John, *Number*: London: Bloomsbury, 1991.

Neugebauer, O. *The Exact Sciences in Antiquity*, New York, Dover 1969

The KJV of the Bible

The Works of Josephus: Complete and Unabridged, New Updated Edition, Translated by William Whiston, Peabody, Mass, Hendrickson, 1987.

DISCLAIMER

While every care has been taken in the compilation of this book, neither the author nor the publisher nor the editor can accept responsibility for errors or omissions. Where such errors or omissions occur and are brought to our attention, they will be corrected for future editions of this book.

Printed in Great Britain
by Amazon

55888320R00028